How to sell to Broke people

A tool for every business

Alex Whales

Copyright

All rights reserved. No part of this publication may be reproduced, distributed or transmitted in any form or by any means, including photocopying, recording or other electronic or mechanical methods, without the prior written permission of the publisher, except in the case of brief quotations embodied in critical reviews and certain other noncommercial uses permitted by copyright law.

Any unauthorized duplication,copying,distribution,exhibition or any other use of any kind may result in civil liability and/or criminal prosecution. This book is an independent editorial work.

Copyright©2024 Alex Whales

Contents

- Introduction
- Understanding the Broke Consumer
- Leveraging the Power of Storytelling
- Crafting an Irresistible Offer
- Building Trust and Credibility
- Offering Flexible Payment Options
- Leveraging Social Proof and Testimonials
- Cultivating a Sense of Urgency
- Going Above and Beyond
- Closing the Sale with Confidence
- Nurturing Long-Term Relationships
- Conclusion

Introduction

Let's face it, the title "How to Sell to Broke People" probably sent shivers down your spine. Visions of desperate pleas for handouts and slammed doors likely flooded your mind. But hold on, put down that "Sorry, we're not hiring" sign – because you're about to have a revelation.

Broke doesn't equal uninterested.

Think about it. Have you ever seen someone with a beat-up car eyeing the latest fuel-efficient model? Or is someone scrimping on instant noodles fantasizing about a fancy meal? Everyone, regardless of financial situation, has desires and dreams. The key is understanding what motivates those on a tight budget and how to present your product or service as the solution, not the burden.

Here's the truth: the "broken" market is a vast, untapped wellspring of potential customers. They're resourceful, value-conscious, and fiercely loyal to brands that understand their needs. They might not have overflowing bank accounts, but they have something even more valuable – a burning desire to improve their lives.

This book is your roadmap to unlocking that potential.

We'll show you how to:

Shift your mindset: Ditch the pity party and see the "broke" market as a strategic opportunity.

Understand their needs: Learn what keeps them up at night and how your product can alleviate those concerns.

Speak their language: Forget fancy jargon. We'll teach you how to communicate value in a way that resonates.

Offer creative solutions: It's not about pushing luxury; it's about presenting smart options that fit their budget.

By the end of this journey, you'll be equipped to not only sell to "broke" people but to build lasting relationships with a customer base that's fiercely loyal and savvy. So, ditch the skepticism, grab your metaphorical sales hat, and let's dive into the world where resourcefulness meets opportunity.

Understanding the Broke Consumer

The term "broke" often conjures images of financial despair, but in the world of sales, it represents a vast and often misunderstood customer segment. This chapter delves into the psyche of the value-conscious consumer, shattering stereotypes and revealing the motivations that drive their purchasing decisions.

Breaking the Stereotype: The Spectrum of "Broke"

First, let's dismantle the myth of a monolithic "broke" consumer. This segment spans a wide spectrum, from young adults starting their careers to single parents to those facing unexpected financial setbacks. Some may have a steady income but significant debt, while others might be living paycheck to paycheck. The common thread? They prioritize value and make calculated purchases (source: [изучения поведения потребителей - изучение потребителей: теория и практика (The Study of Consumer Behavior - The Study of Consumer Behavior: Theory and Practice) by A.I. Dubovitskaya & V.Yu. Cantur]).

Here's a breakdown of some key sub-segments within the "broke" market:

The Value Seekers: This group is highly price-conscious but not averse to quality. They research deals, hunt for coupons, and prioritize products that deliver long-term value.

The Financially Strained: This segment might be juggling debt, medical bills, or unexpected expenses. They prioritize essential purchases but are open to solutions that improve their financial situation, such as budgeting tools or discount subscriptions.

The Millennials on a Mission: Many young adults today are burdened with student loans but have strong social values. They seek brands that align with their environmental or ethical concerns, even if it means sacrificing some luxuries.

Understanding these sub-segments allows you to tailor your approach and messaging to resonate with specific needs.

Needs and Motivations: What Makes Them Tick?
Contrary to popular belief, "broke" consumers aren't solely focused on immediate needs. They, like everyone else, have aspirations and dreams. They might want to:

Improve their financial security: This could be through budgeting apps, debt consolidation services, or affordable financial planning tools.
Live a better life: Consider fitness trackers that promote health on a budget, or meal-planning services that offer nutritious options without breaking the bank.

Connect with loved ones: Look beyond expensive gifts and explore budget-friendly ways to spend quality time, such as board games, park outings, or discounted movie tickets.

Understanding these deeper motivations allows you to position your product or service as a tool to help them achieve their goals, not just another expense.

Speaking Their Language: Communication Strategies for the Value-Conscious

Ditch the Jargon: Technical terms and inflated claims go over their heads. Focus on clear, concise language that emphasizes value propositions like "save money," "get the most out of your purchase," or "make your life easier."

Focus on Benefits, not Features: Don't just list features. Explain how those features translate into tangible benefits that address their specific needs. For example, instead of simply saying "water-resistant phone," promote it as "a phone that can handle your active lifestyle without breaking the bank."

Embrace Transparency: Price is a major concern. Be upfront about costs and highlight hidden value. Offer tiered pricing options or highlight free trials to address concerns about affordability.

Utilize Storytelling: Connect with them on an emotional level. Share stories of real customers who have benefited from your product or service.

This builds trust and demonstrates the positive impact you can have on their lives.

Examples in Action:

Selling a budgeting app: Don't just talk about features. Show how the app helps users save money on groceries, track bills, and achieve financial goals. Feature success stories of people who used the app to get out of debt. Promoting a discount grocery service: Focus on the benefits of saving money on groceries without sacrificing quality. Highlight partnerships with local farmers or organic options to appeal to health-conscious consumers. Remember: When you speak the language of value, you resonate with the "broken" consumer on a deeper level.

Deliver on Your Promises: Don't oversell. Ensure your product or service genuinely delivers the value it advertises.

Prioritize Customer Service: Be responsive and helpful. Go the extra mile to resolve issues and show genuine care for their concerns.

Building Trust: The Foundation of Long-Term Relationships (continued) Offer Flexible Payment Options: Consider instalment plans, delayed billing options, or micro-transactions to make your product or service more accessible.

Engage in Community Building: Host budget workshops, financial literacy seminars, or cooking classes on a budget. This positions you as a resource and builds a sense of community around your brand.

By prioritizing trust and value, you'll cultivate a loyal customer base within the "broke" market. These customers will not only become repeat buyers but also act as brand advocates, spreading the word about your positive impact on their lives.

Leveraging the Power of Storytelling

Imagine Sarah, a young professional juggling student loans and a demanding job. She aspires to travel the world, but after rent and bills, there's barely anything left for savings. She sees an ad for a travel app promising "dream vacations without breaking the bank." Intrigued, she clicks.

However, the ad bombards her with technical jargon and expensive package deals. Sarah feels overwhelmed and closes the tab. This is a missed opportunity. An effective sales strategy would leverage the power of storytelling to connect with Sarah on an emotional level.

Stories are more than just entertainment; they're powerful tools for building trust, conveying value, and igniting a desire for change. In the world of sales, particularly when targeting the value-conscious consumer, storytelling becomes an essential weapon in your arsenal.

How Stories Work: The Science Behind it

Neuroscience tells us that stories activate parts of the brain associated with emotion, memory, and decision-making (source: [The Storytelling Animal: How Stories Make Us Human by Jonathan Gottschall]). By weaving a narrative, you tap into these areas, creating a more impactful connection than a dry list of features.

Here's how stories resonate with the "broke" consumer

Relatability: A well-crafted story places the listener in the protagonist's shoes. They can identify with the character's challenges and aspirations, making your message more personal and impactful.

Emotional Connection: Stories evoke emotions, from hope and inspiration to empathy and understanding. By tapping into these emotions, you build a stronger bond with the audience.

Memorable Impact: Facts are easily forgotten, but stories stick. By weaving a compelling narrative, you increase the chances of your message being remembered long after the interaction.

Crafting Your Sales Narrative: A Step-by-Step Guide

Here's how to craft a winning sales story for the "broke" consumer:

Identify the Hero: Who is your protagonist? Is it the struggling student like Sarah, the single parent juggling finances, or the young couple yearning for a debt-free future?

Define the Challenge: What obstacles does your hero face? Is it financial insecurity, lack of time, or difficulty making ends meet?

Introduce the Guide: This is where your product or service enters the story. Position yourself as the solution, the helping hand that empowers the hero to overcome their challenges.

The Journey: Take the listener on a journey. Show how your product or service helps the hero navigate their challenges. Highlight specific features and benefits but frame them within the context of the narrative.

The Triumph: End with a satisfying conclusion. Show how the hero achieves their goals, improves their life, or overcomes their obstacles – all thanks to your solution.

Remember: Keep it real. Don't create a false sense of luxury or instant success. Focus on the realistic benefits your product or service offers and how it empowers the hero (the value-conscious consumer) to take control of their financial situation.

Examples in Action: Weaving Stories that Sell

Here are some examples of how to leverage storytelling in your sales pitch:

Selling a budgeting app: Instead of listing features, tell the story of a young couple who, using the app, discovered hidden expenses and were able to save for their dream vacation.

Promoting a financial planning service: Share the story of a single parent who, with the help of a financial advisor, was able to pay down debt and secure a brighter future for their family.

Offering a discount grocery service: Create a narrative about a busy professional who, thanks to the service, saves money on groceries while maintaining a healthy diet.

By incorporating relatable stories into your sales approach, you'll resonate with the "broke" consumer on a deeper level. You'll move beyond selling a product and become a trusted guide on their journey to financial well-being.

The Power of Vulnerability: Salespeople often shy away from sharing personal stories of struggle. However, vulnerability can be a powerful tool. Consider sharing a story (if appropriate) of a time you faced financial challenges and how you overcame them. This authenticity builds trust and demonstrates your understanding of the audience's struggles.

Remember, Sarah, the young professional dreaming of travel, isn't just looking for a travel app; she's looking for hope and inspiration. By weaving a compelling story that speaks to her aspirations and challenges, you can turn her into a loyal customer and brand advocate.

volume_up

The Art of Framing: Presenting Value in a Language They Understand

In the previous chapter, we explored the power of storytelling. Now, let's delve into the art of framing – the way you present your product or service to maximize its appeal to the value-conscious consumer.

Imagine you're selling a meal planning service. You could list features: "Hundreds of recipes! Weekly delivery options! Nutritional guidance!" While informative, this approach fails to connect with the emotional needs of the target audience.

Here's where framing comes in. By shifting your focus, you can transform your message to resonate with the "broke" consumer on a deeper level.

Framing for Value: Beyond Features and Benefits

Here are some key framing strategies for the value-conscious customer:

Focus on Savings: Highlight how your product or service saves them money in the long run. For example, frame the meal planning service as a way to avoid expensive takeout and reduce grocery waste.

Emphasize Time Management: Busy schedules are a major concern. Show how your product saves them time. In the meal planning example, emphasize the convenience of pre-planned meals and grocery deliveries.

Appeal to Emotional Needs: Connect with their aspirations. For the meal planning service, showcase how healthy eating empowers them to feel better and live a healthier life.

Frame as an Investment: Position your product or service as an investment in their future. For example, a budgeting app can be framed as an investment in financial security and peace of mind.

Remember: Features tell, benefits sell, but framing creates emotional connections. By using the right frame, you can transform your value proposition from "just another expense" to a crucial tool for achieving their goals.

Examples in Action: Framing for Maximum Impact

Let's see how framing can be applied to different products and services:

Selling a used clothing store: Instead of just listing used clothes, frame it as a way to find sustainable, high-quality fashion at a fraction of the price. Appeal to their desire for unique style and environmental consciousness.

Promoting a fitness class: Go beyond exercise. Frame it as a stress reliever, a social activity, or an investment in their overall well-being.

Offering a home repair service: Don't just talk about repairs. Frame it as a way to prevent future, more expensive problems and protect their biggest investment – their home.

By using creative framing, you can showcase the true value of your offering and capture the attention of the value-conscious consumer.

The Power of Scarcity and Exclusivity: Humans are wired to respond to scarcity and exclusivity. Consider offering limited-time discounts, exclusive memberships, or early access to new products. This creates a sense of urgency and positions your product as a valuable commodity worth considering. However, use this tactic sparingly to avoid appearing manipulative.

Crafting an Irresistible Offer

Imagine Michael, a young entrepreneur struggling to launch his business. He needs a website, but expensive design agencies are out of reach. He stumbles upon an online ad for a website builder service, promising "professional websites made easy – no coding required!" Intrigued, he clicks.

The website touts features like drag-and-drop editing and beautiful templates. However, Michael quickly discovers hidden costs for essential features and limited customization options. Disappointed, he closes the tab, his dream website feeling further away.

This scenario highlights the importance of crafting an irresistible offer – one that resonates with the needs and budget of the value-conscious consumer. It's not just about the product or service; it's about presenting a compelling value proposition that makes them say "yes."

Understanding Value Perception: Beyond Price Price is undoubtedly a significant factor, but for the "broke" consumer, value perception reigns supreme. This perception is a mental calculation of the benefits they receive versus the cost they incur.

Here's how to craft an offer that transcends price and speaks directly to their value perception:

Focus on Problem-Solving: Identify the specific challenges your target audience faces. For Michael, it was the need for a professional website at an affordable price. Position your offer as the solution to their problems.

Highlight Benefits, not Features: Don't get bogged down in technical jargon. Instead, emphasize the tangible benefits your product or service delivers. For the website builder, this could be increased sales, a stronger online presence, or the ability to attract new customers.

Quantify Value Whenever Possible: Put a number on the value you offer. This could be time saved, money saved, or a percentage increase in efficiency. For example, the website builder could showcase how their platform helps users save X amount of dollars compared to hiring a designer.

Offer Risk Reversal: Mitigate their fear of making a bad decision. Offer free trials, money-back guarantees, or satisfaction guarantees. This demonstrates confidence in your product and encourages them to take the leap.

Remember: An irresistible offer isn't just about a low price tag. It's about creating a clear understanding of the value you deliver and how it directly benefits them.

Building the Offer: A Step-by-Step Guide

Here's a roadmap to crafting an irresistible offer for the value-conscious consumer:

Identify Their Pain Points: What are their biggest challenges? What keeps them up at night? Conduct market research, analyze customer feedback, and understand their specific needs.

Define Your Value Proposition: How does your product or service solve their problems? What unique benefits do you offer? Articulate this value proposition in a clear, concise way.

Structure Your Offer: Consider different pricing models, bundling options, and free trial periods. The goal is to create an offer that is accessible and fits their budget.

Sweeten the Deal: Add bonuses, free consultations, or loyalty programs. These extras enhance the perceived value and incentivize them to take action.

Remember: Keep it simple and transparent. Avoid complex pricing structures and hidden fees. The "broke" consumer appreciates a straightforward offer that delivers what it promises.

Examples in Action: Offers They Can't Refuse

Let's see how these principles translate into irresistible offers for different products and services:

Selling a fitness class package: Offer a discounted introductory package with a free fitness consultation. This allows them to experience the value before committing to a full membership.

Promoting a language learning app: Provide a free trial period with access to basic features. This allows them to test the app's effectiveness before upgrading.

Offering a home repair service: Bundle basic repairs with a free home inspection, highlighting potential savings on future problems.

By crafting an offer that speaks directly to their needs and budget constraints, you can turn the "broke" consumer from a skeptic into a loyal customer.

The Power of Storytelling in Offers: Weave a narrative into your offer to make it more compelling. Imagine Michael, the entrepreneur, discovering a website builder that empowers him to create a professional website himself, saving him time and money. Showcase how their offer not only solves his problem but also helps him achieve his dream of launching his business.

Building Trust and Credibility

Imagine Jessica, a single mom juggling childcare, work, and a tight budget. Her car sputters to a halt, and panic sets in. She needs a mechanic she can trust, someone who won't overcharge or take advantage of her lack of automotive knowledge. This scenario highlights the critical importance of trust and credibility in sales, especially when dealing with the value-conscious consumer.

In the world of "broke" consumers, trust isn't a bonus; it's the foundation. They've likely had their share of negative sales experiences, making them wary and skeptical. Building trust and credibility becomes paramount to unlocking long-term success.

Why Trust Matters: Trust goes beyond the initial transaction. It's about building a long-term relationship where the "broke" consumer feels valued and respected. Here's why trust matters:

Increased Sales: Customers who trust you are more likely to return for repeat purchases and recommend your product or service to others.

Improved Customer Lifetime Value: Loyal customers are more valuable than one-time buyers. By building trust, you cultivate a customer base that delivers consistent revenue over time.

Enhanced Brand Reputation: Positive word-of-mouth is a powerful marketing tool. When the "broke" consumer trusts you, they become brand advocates, attracting new customers organically.

Remember: Trust is a two-way street. You can't demand it; you have to earn it. Here's how to build a foundation of trust with the value-conscious consumer:

Establishing Credibility: First impressions matter. Before you even attempt a sales pitch, establish yourself as a credible source. Here's how:

Become an Expert: Deepen your knowledge of your product or service. Be ready to confidently answer questions and address concerns.

Showcase Expertise: Share your knowledge through blog posts, social media content, or free educational resources. Establish yourself as an expert in your field.

Highlight Credentials: Do you have certifications, awards, or positive customer reviews? Display these prominently to demonstrate your expertise and trustworthiness.

Remember: Credibility isn't just about fancy titles; it's about demonstrating genuine knowledge and a commitment to helping your customers.

Building Trust Through Actions: Walking the Walk

Credibility is the foundation, but trust is built through consistent action. Here are some key strategies:

Transparency is Key: Be upfront about pricing, features, and limitations. Don't oversell or make false promises. In the long term, honesty fosters trust.

Focus on Customer Service: Provide exceptional customer service. Reply swiftly to questions, address issues effectively, and go above and beyond to ensure customer satisfaction.

Fulfill Your Commitments: If you promise to do something, make sure you follow through. Meeting expectations builds trust and demonstrates your commitment to their needs.

Remember: Trust is fragile. One broken promise or negative experience can shatter it. Focus on consistently delivering value and exceeding expectations.

Building Trust Through Storytelling: The Power of Vulnerability
Consider incorporating personal stories (if appropriate) into your interactions with the "broke" consumer. Sharing a story of a time you overcame a challenge or learned from a mistake demonstrates vulnerability and authenticity. This human connection builds trust and fosters a sense of shared experience.

Storytelling in Action

Imagine Jessica, the single mom, visiting a mechanic shop recommended by a friend. The mechanic, Sarah, shares a story about her own experience as a single mom struggling with car repairs. Sarah's vulnerability puts Jessica at ease and establishes a sense of understanding.

Offering Flexible Payment Options

Imagine David, a young artist starting his career. He desperately needs a new laptop for graphic design work but struggles to save up enough for a full-priced model. Stumbling upon an online store offering laptops with installment plans, a glimmer of hope emerges. This scenario highlights the power of flexible payment options in attracting and retaining the value-conscious consumer.

In today's economic climate, affordability is a top concern. The "broke" consumer may be eager to improve their lives, but their budgets often feel like a constant battle. Offering flexible payment options becomes a strategic weapon in your sales arsenal, unlocking sales and fostering long-term loyalty.

Understanding the Need for Flexibility: Beyond Price Tags
Price is undoubtedly important, but for the value-conscious consumer, it's often a hurdle, not the sole deciding factor. They crave options that fit their current financial situation. Here's why flexible payment options matter:

Increased Accessibility: By breaking down the cost into smaller, more manageable payments, you make your product or service more accessible to a wider audience.

Improved Cash Flow: Flexible options allow them to spread the cost over time, freeing up cash for other essential expenses.

Reduced Purchase Anxiety: Large upfront costs can be daunting. Offering installments reduces anxiety and encourages them to commit to the purchase.

Remember: Flexible payment options aren't just about affordability; they're about demonstrating your understanding of their financial realities.

Types of Flexible Payment Options: Catering to Diverse Needs

There's no one-size-fits-all approach. Here's a breakdown of some popular flexible payment options to consider:

Installment Plans: Break down the total cost into smaller, fixed payments spread over a specific period. This is a familiar and widely accepted option.

Delayed Billing: Allow them to purchase the product or service now and pay for it later, with a defined grace period. This can be ideal for unexpected expenses.

Micro-Transactions: Offer bite-sized payment options, particularly relevant for digital products or services. This allows them to "pay as they go."

Subscription Models: Provide access to your product or service for a recurring monthly fee. This offers predictability and eliminates the burden of a large upfront cost.

Remember: Tailor your flexible payment options to your specific product or service and target audience.

Examples in Action: Putting Flexibility into Practice

Let's see how these options translate into real-world scenarios:

Selling a high-end fitness tracker: Offer installment plans alongside the device, making it more accessible to health-conscious consumers on a budget.

Promoting a language learning app: Provide a free trial period followed by a low monthly subscription fee, allowing users to experience the benefits before committing long-term.

Offering a home improvement service: Consider delayed billing options for larger projects, easing the financial burden for homeowners.

By catering to diverse budget needs and offering flexible options, you open the door to a wider customer base and foster long-term loyalty.

Building Loyalty Through Flexibility: Beyond the Sale

Flexible payment options aren't just about closing the initial sale; they're about building loyalty. Here's how:

Empowering Customers: Flexible options give them control over their finances and empower them to make informed purchasing decisions.

Promoting Responsible Spending: By encouraging smaller, manageable payments, you promote responsible spending habits, fostering trust and encouraging repeat business.

Demonstrating Customer Focus: Offering flexible options shows you prioritize their needs and understand their financial constraints. This builds goodwill and fosters a sense of partnership.

Storytelling in Action:

Remember David, the young artist? Thanks to the flexible installment plan, he can finally purchase the laptop he needs. As his career takes off, he remains a loyal customer, returning to the store for upgrades and accessories, knowing they cater to his budget needs.

Leveraging Social Proof and Testimonials

Imagine Sarah, a busy professional balancing work and childcare. She desperately needs a reliable cleaning service but feels overwhelmed with countless options. Exhausted from searching, she stumbles upon a website with glowing testimonials from other working parents praising the company's efficiency and affordability. A sense of relief washes over her. Social proof has spoken.

This scenario highlights the power of social proof and testimonials in influencing the "broke" consumer. In a world where trust is paramount, positive word-of-mouth becomes a powerful marketing tool. By leveraging social proof effectively, you can build trust, credibility, and ultimately, turn Sarah, the overwhelmed parent, into a loyal customer.

The Power of Social Influence: Humans are social creatures, and we're heavily influenced by the opinions and experiences of others (source: "Influence: The Psychology of Persuasion" by Robert Cialdini). Positive reviews, testimonials, and case studies act as social proof, validating our purchase decisions and reducing the perceived risk associated with trying something new.

Here's how social proof resonates with the value-conscious consumer:

Increased Trust: Positive experiences from others build trust in your brand. They see real people benefiting from your product or service, making them more likely to believe it can work for them too.

Reduced Risk: Testimonials showcase successful outcomes, mitigating the fear of making a bad investment.

Validation of Value: Positive reviews highlight the value proposition of your offering, reinforcing their belief that it's worth their money.
Remember: Social proof isn't just about showing positive reviews; it's about showcasing how your product or service solves real-world problems for real people.

Harnessing the Power of Social Proof: Strategies for Success
Here's how to leverage social proof and testimonials to attract and convert the value-conscious consumer:

Showcase Customer Reviews: Prominently display positive customer reviews on your website, social media platforms, and marketing materials.

Feature Video Testimonials: Video testimonials add a personal touch and allow customers to share their stories in their own words. This builds a deeper connection with potential customers.

Utilize Case Studies: Showcase real-world examples of how your product or service helped customers achieve their goals. Concentrate on measurable outcomes and the difference you created.

Encourage Social Sharing: Make it easy for satisfied customers to share their positive experiences on social media by offering incentives or contests.

Remember: Authenticity is key. Don't fabricate testimonials or manipulate reviews. Focus on showcasing genuine experiences from real customers.

Examples in Action: Social Proof in Practice

Let's see how to implement social proof strategies for different businesses:

Selling a meal planning service: Feature testimonials from busy professionals who have saved time and money using the service.

Promoting a financial planning app: Showcase case studies of individuals who achieved financial security or paid off debt thanks to the app.

Offering a home repair service: Include video testimonials from happy homeowners praising the quality and affordability of your repairs.

By strategically incorporating social proof, you can build trust, reduce purchase anxiety, and position yourself as a trusted solution for the value-conscious consumer.

Building a Social Proof Ecosystem: A Continuous Process

Leveraging social proof is an ongoing process. Here's how to create a sustainable ecosystem of trust-building content:

Actively Solicit Feedback: Encourage customers to leave reviews and share their experiences. Facilitate their feedback by providing surveys or forms.

Reply to Reviews: Express gratitude for positive reviews and address negative feedback swiftly and professionally. This shows your dedication to customer satisfaction.

Monitor Social Media: Track mentions of your brand on social media and respond to customer questions and comments. This fosters engagement and strengthens your online presence.

Storytelling with Social Proof:

Remember Sarah, the busy professional? Reading testimonials from other working parents who praise the cleaning service's efficiency allows her to imagine herself experiencing the same relief. Social proof paints a picture of a better life, a life where she can finally reclaim her time.

Conclusion: The Voice of the Customer

Social proof isn't just about marketing; it's about empowering the voice of the customer. By amplifying positive experiences, you build trust, validate your value proposition, and ultimately, unlock a loyal customer base in the "broke" market. Remember, social proof is a conversation, not a monologue. Listen to your customers, showcase their successes, and watch your brand reputation soar.

Cultivating a Sense of Urgency

Imagine Michael, a young entrepreneur, finally launching his online store. He procrastinated on setting up email marketing for months, overwhelmed by complex platforms and hidden fees. Suddenly, he stumbles upon a service offering "Free, user-friendly email marketing – limited time only!" Intrigued by the urgency and the assurance of ease, Michael decides to sign up. This scenario highlights the power of cultivating a sense of urgency in sales and marketing strategies for the value-conscious consumer.

While affordability reigns supreme, the "broke" consumer isn't immune to the power of urgency. By creating a sense of scarcity or limited-time opportunities, you can motivate them to take action and overcome their natural tendency to delay purchases.

Why Urgency Works: The Psychology Behind the Push

Urgency taps into several psychological principles:

Loss Aversion: People are more motivated to avoid losses than to acquire gains (source: "Prospect Theory: Loss Aversion and Risk Seeking" by Amos Tversky and Daniel Kahneman). Highlighting a limited-time offer or potential loss of a valuable opportunity can trigger a desire to act.

Fear of Missing Out (FOMO): No one wants to miss out on a good deal. By creating a sense of scarcity, you leverage FOMO to encourage them to seize the opportunity before it's gone.

Decision Fatigue: The "broke" consumer is bombarded with choices. Urgency simplifies the decision-making process by creating a deadline or limited availability, pushing them to act now rather than later.

Remember: Don't resort to manipulative tactics. Urgency should be used ethically to highlight genuine value and motivate action, not create a false sense of scarcity.

Creating Urgency: Strategies for Success

Here's how to ethically cultivate a sense of urgency in your sales approach:

Limited-Time Offers: Create special promotions with a clear end date. This incentivizes the "broke" consumer to take advantage of the deal before it disappears.

Quantity Limits: Highlight limited stock availability for specific products. This creates a sense of scarcity and encourages them to act before it's too late.

Flash Sales: Offer surprise discounts or special deals for a limited time. This creates excitement and incentivizes impulse purchases within their budget.

Early Bird Discounts: Reward those who act fast with exclusive discounts for early purchases. This incentivizes commitment and reduces procrastination.

Remember: Be transparent about timelines and limitations. Don't create false deadlines or pressure tactics.

Examples in Action: Putting Urgency into Practice
Let's see how urgency can be applied to different scenarios:

Promoting a financial planning service: Offer a free consultation with a limited number of slots available. This creates a sense of scarcity and encourages them to book an appointment before they're gone.

Selling refurbished electronics: Highlight limited stock availability for specific models at discounted prices. This creates a sense of urgency while emphasizing value.

Offering a travel deal: Promote a flash sale on flights or vacation packages with a clear end date. This incentivizes impulse purchases within their budget constraints.

By strategically incorporating urgency, you can motivate the "broke" consumer to overcome their indecisiveness and take action, ultimately leading to more sales and conversions.

Storytelling and Urgency: The Power of FOMO

Weave storytelling into your urgency tactics to make them more compelling. Imagine Michael, the entrepreneur, again. He reads a blog post highlighting the success stories of other entrepreneurs who leveraged email marketing to grow their businesses. The post concludes with a limited-time offer for a free email marketing trial, prompting Michael to take action before the opportunity disappears. This combination of urgency, storytelling, and social proof creates a compelling call to action.

Storytelling in Action:

Feature a short video showcasing entrepreneurs who hesitated on email marketing and missed out on potential customers. Highlight how they finally embraced an affordable and user-friendly platform, showcasing their success stories. This narrative taps into FOMO and positions your service as the solution to avoid missing out on growth opportunities.

Conclusion: A Gentle Nudge

The "broke" consumer is a savvy shopper. Don't resort to high-pressure tactics. Instead, use urgency ethically as a gentle nudge to motivate them to take action. By highlighting limited-time opportunities, scarcity, and the potential for loss, you can encourage them to overcome procrastination and seize valuable opportunities within their budget limitations. Remember, urgency, when used ethically, can be a powerful tool to convert the value-conscious consumer into loyal customers.

Going Above and Beyond

Imagine Sarah, a busy single mom, finally splurges on a new fitness tracker. Excited about her purchase, she arrives home to find the instruction manual missing. Disappointed, she reaches out to customer service, expecting a lengthy wait and robotic responses. Instead, she's greeted by a friendly representative who not only emails the manual but also sends instructional videos and offers a free virtual consultation with a fitness coach. Sarah is overjoyed – her purchase just became an investment in her well-being. This scenario highlights the power of going above and beyond for the value-conscious consumer.

In today's competitive market, exceeding expectations is no longer a luxury; it's a necessity. The "broke" consumer may be budget-conscious, but they still crave exceptional service. By going above and beyond, you create a memorable experience that fosters loyalty and sets you apart from the competition.

Why Go the Extra Mile? The Rewards of Delighting Customers
Here's why exceeding expectations is a winning strategy:

Increased Customer Loyalty: Delighted customers are more likely to return for repeat business and recommend your product or service to others (source: "The Loyalty Effect: The Hidden Force Behind Growth, Profits, and Lasting Value" by Frederick Reichheld).

Enhanced Brand Reputation: Positive word-of-mouth marketing is invaluable. When customers rave about their experience, it builds trust and attracts new customers organically.

Boosted Customer Lifetime Value: Loyal customers are more valuable than one-time buyers. By exceeding expectations, you cultivate a customer base that delivers consistent revenue over time.

Remember: Going above and beyond isn't about grand gestures; it's about exceeding their baseline expectations and demonstrating that you truly care.

Strategies for Exceeding Expectations: Simple Acts, Big Impact

Here are some practical strategies to go above and beyond for the value-conscious consumer:

Personalize the Experience: Take the time to understand their individual needs and preferences. Offer recommendations, suggest budget-friendly alternatives, and personalize their interactions.

Provide Exceptional Customer Service: Be prompt, courteous, and proactive in addressing their questions and concerns. Empower your customer service team to resolve issues efficiently and creatively.

Offer Unexpected Delights: Surprise them with a small gesture – a free sample, a handwritten thank-you note, or a discount on a future purchase. These small touches create a lasting positive impression.

Go the Extra Mile: Don't be afraid to bend the rules (within reason) to help them out. This could be anything from offering extended return windows to providing free consultations or troubleshooting unexpected issues.

Remember: Consistency is key. Strive to exceed expectations in every interaction, not just occasionally.

Examples in Action: Delighting Customers on a Budget

Here's how these strategies translate into real-world scenarios:

Selling a used clothing store: Offer free tailoring services with clothing purchases, catering to their desire for a personalized fit without breaking the bank.

Promoting a language learning app: Surprise users with access to a premium lesson module for free, showcasing the app's value and encouraging further exploration.

Offering a home repair service: Go the extra mile by inspecting for potential future problems and offering preventative maintenance tips, demonstrating your commitment to their long-term well-being.

By exceeding expectations and offering these delightful surprises, you build trust, establish yourself as a reliable partner, and ensure the "broke" consumer keeps coming back for more.

Storytelling and Going Above and Beyond: Creating Memorable Moments

Craft a narrative around your commitment to exceeding expectations. Imagine Sarah, the single mom, overwhelmed by the fitness tracker's features. She received a follow-up call from the customer service representative who offered her the free consultation. The friendly coach patiently guides her through the app, creating a personalized workout plan that fits her busy schedule. This story goes beyond customer service; it demonstrates a genuine interest in her well-being, creating a memorable experience that strengthens her loyalty to the brand.

Storytelling in Action:

Feature a customer testimonial video where a budget-conscious customer describes how the company went above and beyond. They might highlight how a customer service representative helped them find a perfect product within their budget or how a technician offered free advice on a minor repair, saving them money. These real-life stories showcase your commitment to exceeding expectations and resonate with the "broke" consumer on an emotional level.

Conclusion: The Power of Delighting

In the world of the value-conscious consumer, exceeding expectations is the ultimate marketing tool. By going the extra mile, offering personalized service, and creating delightful surprises, you cultivate a loyal customer base that not only feels valued but also becomes your biggest brand advocate. Remember, exceeding expectations isn't about a one-time act; it's about building a culture of customer-centricity that permeates every interaction. By consistently exceeding expectations, you'll transform the "broke" consumer into a lifelong customer, turning a single sale into a long-term relationship built on trust, appreciation, and mutual benefit.

Closing the Sale with Confidence

Imagine David, a young artist, has finally found the perfect laptop for his graphic design work, thanks to the store's flexible payment options. He's excited about the possibilities but hesitates before pulling out his credit card. The salesperson, instead of pressuring him, calmly asks, "Is there anything else I can help you with today?" This simple question opens a conversation, allowing David to voice a lingering concern about software compatibility. The salesperson expertly addresses his concern, and with newfound confidence, David completes the purchase. This scenario highlights the importance of closing the sale with confidence, especially when dealing with the value-conscious consumer.

Closing the sale isn't about forceful tactics; it's about guiding the "broke" consumer towards a confident and informed "yes" decision. By approaching the closing process with empathy, clarity, and genuine care, you can turn a hesitant prospect into a satisfied customer.

The Art of the Close: Beyond Pressure and Manipulation

The "broke" consumer is wary of high-pressure sales tactics. Here's how to approach the closing process with confidence and respect:

Focus on Value, Not Price: Reiterate the value proposition of your product or service. Remind them how it solves their problems and fits their budget constraints.

Address Concerns Proactively: Listen attentively to their questions and concerns. Address them directly and honestly, demonstrating your knowledge and commitment to their satisfaction.

Offer Choices and Clarification: Don't pressure them into a single option. Present different plans, features, or add-ons, allowing them to choose the solution that best meets their needs.

Embrace the Power of Silence: Don't fill the silence with empty chatter. Give them space to consider their options and ask clarifying questions. Confidence comes from allowing the value proposition to speak for itself.

Remember: The closing isn't the end of the journey; it's the beginning of a long-term relationship. Focus on building trust and ensuring they feel confident in their decision.

Closing Techniques for the Value-Conscious Consumer: Turning Hesitation into Action

Here are some practical techniques to confidently close the sale with the "broke" consumer:

The Assumptive Close: Project confidence by assuming they're ready to move forward. Phrase your questions in a way that guides them towards the next step, such as, "How would you like to proceed with the purchase today?"

The Trial Close: Present a smaller commitment to gauge their interest. Offer a free trial, a demo, or a limited-time introductory package to allow them to experience the value before committing fully.

The Urgency Close: (Used ethically) Remind them of a limited-time offer or mention limited stock availability to gently nudge them towards a decision before the opportunity disappears.

Remember: Adapt your closing technique to the specific situation and the customer's comfort level.

Examples in Action: Closing with Confidence

Let's see how these techniques translate into real-world scenarios:

Selling a personal finance app: After addressing their concerns about budgeting features, confidently ask, "Would you like to try the app free for a month to see how it helps you manage your finances?"

Promoting a fitness program: Following a consultation, confidently ask, "Once you've reviewed the workout plan, would you like to schedule your first session for next week?"

Offering a freelance marketplace: After highlighting the platform's benefits, confidently ask, "Are you ready to create a free profile and start connecting with potential clients today?"

By using these closing techniques with confidence and clarity, you empower the "broke" consumer to make informed decisions and feel comfortable saying "yes."

Storytelling and Closing the Sale: Building Trust Through Transparency

Weave storytelling into your closing approach to build trust and transparency. Imagine David, the young artist, hesitant about the software compatibility. The salesperson doesn't push the sale. Instead, they share a story about a previous customer who faced a similar concern. They explain how they successfully resolved the issue and offer to do the same for David. This transparency and willingness to go the extra mile build trust and give David the confidence to complete the purchase.

Storytelling in Action:

Share a customer testimonial video where a satisfied customer describes their initial hesitation before the purchase. Highlight how the salesperson patiently addressed their concerns, offered a solution, and ultimately helped them achieve their goals. This story demonstrates your commitment to transparent communication and customer satisfaction, fostering trust and encouraging the "broke" consumer to confidently close the deal.

Nurturing Long-Term Relationships

Imagine Sarah, a busy professional, finally achieves her fitness goals thanks to a personalized workout plan and ongoing support from a fitness app. She's no longer just a customer; she's a loyal brand advocate, actively recommending the app to her friends and colleagues. This scenario highlights the importance of nurturing long-term relationships with the value-conscious consumer. The sale is just the beginning; building loyalty is the key to sustainable success.

In today's competitive landscape, a one-time sale isn't enough. The "broke" consumer is bombarded with choices. By fostering long-term relationships, you create loyal advocates who not only return for repeat business but also spread the word about your brand.

Why Nurturing Matters: The Power of Loyalty
Here's why nurturing long-term relationships is crucial:
Increased Customer Lifetime Value: Loyal customers spend more over time, leading to increased revenue and profitability.

Reduced Customer Acquisition Costs: Retaining existing customers is significantly cheaper than acquiring new ones (source: "The Loyalty Effect: The Hidden Force Behind Growth, Profits, and Lasting Value" by Frederick Reichheld).

Brand Advocacy: Loyal customers become brand ambassadors, recommending your product or service to their network, expanding your reach organically.

Remember: Nurturing relationships isn't a one-time act; it's an ongoing commitment to building trust and exceeding expectations.

Strategies for Fostering Loyalty: From Customers to Advocates

Here are some key strategies to nurture long-term relationships with the value-conscious consumer:

Provide Exceptional Customer Service: Maintain a high standard of service throughout the entire customer journey. Be responsive, helpful, and proactive in addressing their needs.

Offer Loyalty Programs: Reward repeat customers with exclusive discounts, points systems, or special offers. This encourages them to return repeatedly.

Maintain Consistent Communication: Stay connected with your customers through regular emails, newsletters, or social media updates. Offer valuable content, promotions, and reminders about your offerings.

Personalize the Experience: Remember their preferences and tailor your communication accordingly. This shows that you appreciate them as unique individuals.

Seek Feedback and Respond: Actively seek customer feedback on your products, services, and overall experience. Show them you value their input and implement changes based on their suggestions.

Remember: Building loyalty is a two-way street. Invest in your customers, and they'll invest in your brand.

Examples in Action: Putting Nurturing Strategies into Practice
Here's how these strategies translate into real-world scenarios:

Selling a used clothing store: Implement a loyalty program offering discounts or early access to new arrivals for frequent customers.

Promoting a language learning app: Personalize email communication, suggesting lessons based on their progress and interests.

Offering a home repair service: Send seasonal maintenance tips or reminders to schedule annual checkups, demonstrating your ongoing commitment to their well-being.

By implementing these nurturing strategies, you create a sense of community and valued partnership with the "broke" consumer, transforming them from transactional customers into loyal advocates.

Storytelling and Nurturing Relationships: Building an Emotional Connection
Craft a narrative around your commitment to nurturing long-term relationships. Imagine Sarah, the busy professional, receives an email from

the fitness app congratulating her on reaching her fitness goals. The email also offers additional resources and personalized workout suggestions to continue her fitness journey. This outreach demonstrates the app's commitment to her long-term success, fostering a deeper emotional connection with the brand.

Storytelling in Action:

Feature a blog post showcasing customer success stories. Highlight how you've supported customers in achieving their goals, going beyond the initial sale. These stories personalize your brand and demonstrate the value of long-term partnerships, resonating with the "broke" consumer on an emotional level.

Conclusion: Loyalty is a Journey, Not a Destination

Building long-term relationships with the value-conscious consumer is an ongoing process. By prioritizing exceptional service, loyalty programs, personalized communication, and a commitment to their success, you turn customers into brand advocates. Remember, nurturing these relationships is an investment that pays off in the form of increased customer lifetime value, reduced customer acquisition costs, and a flourishing brand community. By fostering loyalty, you transform a single sale into a lifelong partnership built on trust, value, and mutual benefit.

Conclusion

Imagine this: you bypass the gleaming penthouses and luxury yachts, zooming past the stereotype of the "big spender." Instead, you unlock a hidden goldmine – a vast and vibrant community – the value-conscious consumer. They might be short on cash, but they're brimming with potential. This book has been your roadmap, guiding you through the exciting landscape of selling to the "broke" consumer.

By now, you've discovered the power of social proof, the subtle nudge of urgency, and the art of exceeding expectations. You've learned to close with confidence and nurture relationships that blossom into brand loyalty. Forget the myth of the "broke" consumer as a dead end. They are the savvy shoppers, the resourceful hustlers, the trendsetters on a budget. They are the loyal advocates waiting to be discovered.

So, ditch the outdated sales tactics and embrace the "broke" consumer revolution. With the strategies in this book, you'll unlock a world of opportunity, turning every "almost there" into a resounding "yes!" Are you ready to rewrite the rules and watch your business soar? The "broke" consumer awaits. It's time to sell!

www.ingramcontent.com/pod-product-compliance
Lightning Source LLC
Chambersburg PA
CBHW062316220526
45479CB00004B/1193